CORAL REEFS

HIDDEN COLONIES OF THE SEA

JENNY WOOD

Gareth Stevens Children's Books
MILWAUKEE

Wonderworks of Nature:

Caves: An Underground Wonderland
Coral Reefs: Hidden Colonies of the Sea
Deserts: An Arid Wilderness
Icebergs: Titans of the Oceans
Rain Forests: Lush Tropical Paradise
Storms: Nature's Fury
Volcanoes: Fire from Below
Waterfalls: Nature's Thundering Splendor

For a free color catalog describing Gareth Stevens' list of high-quality children's books, call 1-800-341-3569 (USA) or 1-800-461-9120 (Canada).

Picture Credits:
Ardea — 5, 6 (top and bottom left), 7, 11, 14 (top); Bruce Coleman — 6-7, 12-13, 14 (bottom), 18, 21; Robert Harding — 15, 20; Oxford Scientific Films — 17 (top), 22, 23; Planet Earth Pictures — front and back covers, 9, 16 (top); Zefa — 10, 16 (bottom), 17 (bottom)

Illustration Credits:
All illustrations by Francis Mosley except pp. 24-28, Martin Salisbury/Linda Rogers Associates
Line art: Keith Ward

Library of Congress Cataloging-in-Publication Data

Wood, Jenny.
    Coral reefs : hidden colonies of the sea / Jenny Wood.
        p.   cm. — (Wonderworks of nature)
    Includes index.
    Summary: Describes what coral reefs are, how and where they are formed, and what sorts of life-forms inhabit them.
    ISBN 0-8368-0630-1
    1. Coral reef ecology—Juvenile literature. 2. Coral reefs and islands—Juvenile literature. [1. Coral reef ecology. 2. Coral reefs and islands.] I. Title. II. Series: Wood, Jenny. Wonderworks of nature.
QH541.5.C7W66   1991
574.5'26367—dc20   91-17703

This North American edition first published in 1991 by
Gareth Stevens Children's Books
1555 North RiverCenter Drive, Suite 201
Milwaukee, Wisconsin 53212, USA

This U.S. edition copyright © 1991. First published in the United Kingdom by Two-Can Publishing, Ltd. Text copyright © 1991 by Jenny Wood.

Printed in the United States of America

2 3 4 5 6 7 8 9 97 96 95 94 93

CONTENTS

All words in **boldface** can be found in the glossary.

WHAT IS A CORAL REEF?

Huge reefs, or ridges, of orange, yellow, and purple coral thrive in the clear, shallow waters of the world's warm seas. The corals come in all forms, shaped like branching trees, tiny pipes, or saucers. They are ridges of limestone, formed by millions of tiny animals called coral polyps.

The polyps that build the reefs are known as stony corals. They live in groups called colonies. **Cells** on the outside of the polyps' bodies collect a chemical called calcium carbonate from the seawater. Calcium carbonate hardens to form limestone, and this grows into a protective shell around each polyp. When the polyps die, their shells remain. As new polyps grow on the old limestone shells, the reef becomes larger.

▶ Coral reefs are often described as underwater gardens. They are colorful, fascinating places and provide a home for many sea creatures.

A new coral reef begins with a single, tiny polyp called a **planula**. Planulae are produced from the eggs of some types of female stony coral polyps that have been fertilized by **sperm** from a male polyp. They swim through the water until they find a hard surface on which to rest. A planula begins to produce limestone as soon as it is settled.

Tentacles carry food into the polyp's body

Mouth - through which the polyp takes in food and gets rid of waste materials

Eggs floating away

Female polyp

Male polyp

A cup-shaped shell of hard limestone forms around the lower half of a stony coral polyp's body

A coral polyp's tube-shaped body is made of a jelly-like material

Planulae

Once the building of a new reef has been started, the polyps begin to bud. Small, knoblike growths appear on the body of each adult polyp. These gradually develop into independent polyps, and so the reef begins to increase in size.

1

2

3

4

A CLOSER LOOK AT CORAL

There are more than 2,500 **species** of coral. About 650 of these are the reef-building stony corals whose limestone shells and skeletons form the basic structure of a coral reef. But other types of coral grow on or near a reef, too, although their colonies are smaller in size. These are the colorful soft corals.

Soft corals do not produce limestone shells to protect their bodies. Instead, they have hornlike skeletons strengthened by

tiny needles of limestone called **spicules**. Soft corals can bend and sway in the water.

▼ Corals come in a huge variety of colors. Some are very bright, like this cave coral, and some are even fluorescent.

▶ Gorgonian corals develop colonies made up of long, thin branches that sway in the ocean **currents**. These corals have an internal skeleton made out of a material called gorgonin.

◀ Can you see the mouths of these hard coral polyps?

▼ Coral polyps eat tiny sea creatures known as **zooplankton**. The polyps capture food with stinging tentacles that stun the zooplankton as they come near a polyp. The tentacles then carry the zooplankton into the polyp's mouth.

WHERE CORAL REEFS ARE FOUND

Reef-building stony corals cannot live in water that is colder than 61°F (16°C), so the world's coral reefs are found in the warm seas that lie on either side of the equator. Corals usually develop in clear, shallow water that is no more than 150 feet (46 m) deep, so many coral reefs are situated near land.

Scientists believe that the stony corals choose clear, shallow water to develop in because of their special relationship with tiny **algae** known as **zooxanthellae**.

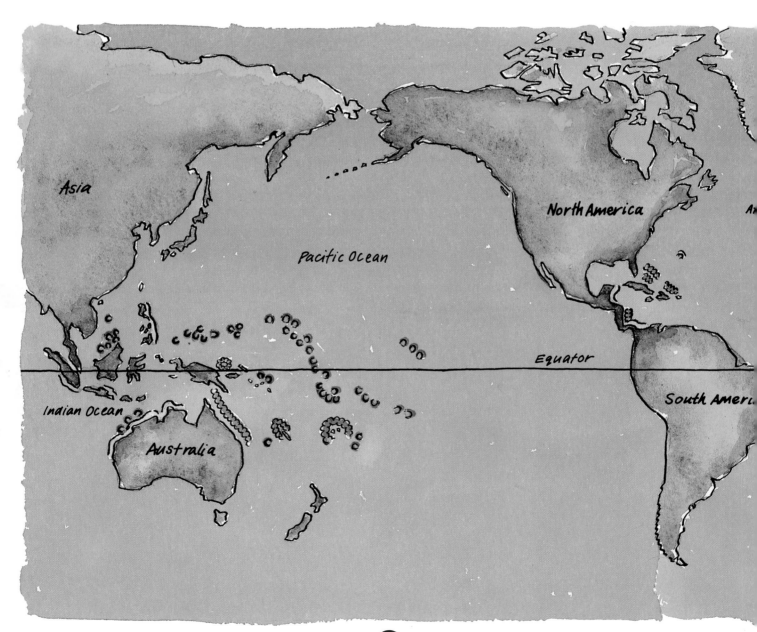

Zooxanthellae live inside the cells of the coral polyps' bodies. They use energy from sunlight to make food and, as they do this, provide the polyps with nourishment. Sunlight does not reach into deep ocean water, so the zooxanthellae need to remain close to the water's surface. The polyps, in turn, need the food provided by the zooxanthellae, so they must also stay in shallow water.

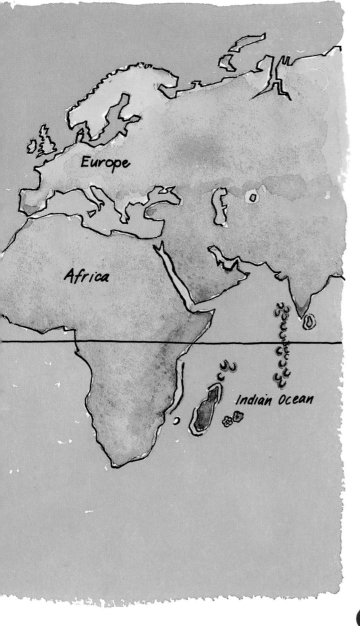

▲ Many different types of coral live clustered together. These corals are in the Red Sea.

◀ The world's coral reefs.
Key to map

~~~~~~ **Fringe reef**
〰〰〰 **Barrier reef**
🜂🜂🜂 **Coral atoll**

FRINGE REEFS AND BARRIER REEFS

Fringe reefs form a border, or fringe, of coral along a shoreline. They grow on the shelves of rock that extend from the shores of islands or continents into the sea. A fringe reef is separated from the land by a narrow stretch of water that is shallow enough to wade across when the tide is out.

Barrier reefs also grow parallel to the land, but are separated from

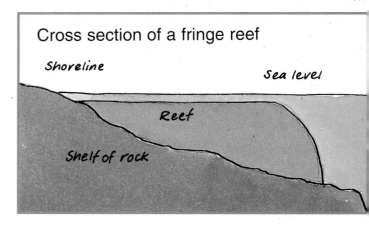

Cross section of a fringe reef

Shoreline

Sea level

Reef

Shelf of rock

▼ It is easy to see coral under clear water.

the shoreline by a larger area of calm water called a **lagoon**. Reefs act as barriers between the lagoon and the waters of the open sea.

The world's largest and best-known barrier reef is the Great Barrier Reef, off the northeastern coast of Australia. It stretches for 1,260 miles (2,027 km), and parts of it lie over 100 miles (160 km) from the coast. Like most barrier reefs, the Great Barrier Reef is made up of smaller reefs separated by channels of water.

▶ Heron Island is one of the thousands of islands with fringe reefs that form part of Australia's Great Barrier Reef.

DID YOU KNOW?

● The Great Barrier Reef is the largest known single structure ever built by living creatures.

● About four hundred different species of coral grow on the Great Barrier Reef.

● Scientists believe that the Great Barrier Reef began forming thirty million years ago.

● The bottom of the Great Barrier Reef lies over 492 feet (150 m) below the water's surface, over three times deeper than reef-building corals usually grow. Scientists believe that the reef was originally a fringe reef that sank as the earth's crust moved and lowered the level of the seabed.

CORAL ATOLLS

Coral atolls are the most unusual type of reef. An atoll is a ring of coral that surrounds nothing but water.

The nineteenth-century scientist Charles Darwin was the first person to explain how atolls developed. He believed that an atoll started life as a fringe reef surrounding a **volcanic island**. Over thousands of years, movements in the earth's **crust** caused changes in the level of the ocean floor. The volcanic island and its surrounding reef slowly began to sink. New coral kept forming on the top of the reef, so when the island was covered by the sea, only the reef remained.

metimes coral atolls develop into
l islands. A thin layer of sand
rs the reef, and trees and plants
from seeds carried by birds or
wind.

laldive Islands in the Indian Ocean are
atolls. Most coral islands are no more
:0 feet (6 m) high, and some are less
yard (1 m) above the water. They are
stant danger of being flooded by heavy
:aused by tropical storms. ▼

The development of a coral atoll:

1 A fringe reef grows around a volcanic island.

2 As the island begins to sink, the stretch of water between it and the coral reef widens. The reef is now a barrier reef.

3 The island disappears completely beneath the surface, and a coral atoll now surrounds a shallow lagoon. Channels between the stretches of coral connect the lagoon with the open sea.

CORAL-REEF CREATURES

Coral reefs are full of creatures. At least two thousand different species have been recorded in just one area of the Great Barrier Reef.

Most coral-reef fish are brilliantly colored. Many have unusual shapes and are decorated with stripes, spots, and other markings. These markings allow them to blend in with their surroundings and hide easily from their enemies.

Many of the creatures and plants that live in and around a coral reef depend on each other for food and shelter. A special relationship exists between the

▲ The harlequin tusk fish has teeth like tusks outside its mouth.

▶ This anemone is surrounded by clown fish and damsel fish.

clown fish and the sea anemone. The swaying tentacles of the sea anemone release poison at the slightest touch. But the clown fish are not harmed by the poison. They lay their eggs near the anemone's base and rear their young among the swaying tentacles. They leave this shelter only to find food. The anemone benefits from the partnership by eating the leftovers of the clown fish's meals. The clown fish may also attract other fish to the anemone, which the anemone then eats.

▲ Angelfish are among the most colorful reef-dwelling fish. They have narrow, streamlined bodies, and they dart easily through the coral.

SPONGES AND STARFISH

Many creatures other than fish make their home on a coral reef. Starfish and prickly sea urchins move slowly across the reef, using the suckers on the undersides of their bodies to grip the surface. Fierce marine snails hide their soft bodies within beautifully patterned shells. Clams and oysters lie buried in the sand or attached to the reef limestone, opening their shells from time to time to take in food. Colorful crabs hide in the nooks and crannies of the reef, and tiny shrimp swim through the shallow water. Sponges of all shapes, colors, and sizes live in the coral **habitat**.

▲ The blue starfish grows up to 16 inches (41 cm) from the tip of one arm to the tip of another.

◀ Under each arm, a starfish has a row of suction disks that it uses to move along the coral. At the tip of each arm is an eyespot that is sensitive to light, although the starfish moves more by touch than sight.

Some of the reef creatures grow to a huge size. Giant clams, for example, can measure over 5 feet (1.5 m) in length and weigh more than 500 pounds (225 kg). They feed on tiny plants and animals that they filter from the seawater.

DID YOU KNOW?

● A starfish's favorite meal is a shellfish such as a clam or oyster. The starfish wraps itself around the shellfish, places its mouth over the seam between the two shells, and pulls hard. As the shells begin to come apart, the starfish turns its stomach inside out through its mouth and pushes it through the opening. The starfish's stomach surrounds the shellfish's soft body and gobbles it up!

● If a starfish loses part of its body during a fight with another underwater creature, the lost body part will grow again. The blue starfish can grow a whole new body from just a single arm and part of its central disk.

▲ Sea horses belong to a group of fish known as "tubemouths." They hold themselves steady in the water by hooking their tails around the coral.

▶ There are more than five thousand different species of sponges. Sponges are animals that attach themselves to the hard surface of the reef. They feed by drawing water into their bodies, then filtering out the tiny plants and animals that they eat.

CORAL IN DANGER

A giant starfish known as the crown-of-thorns has caused terrible destruction to many of the world's coral reefs. The crown-of-thorns eats coral polyps. But instead of nibbling small areas and leaving enough living coral for new polyps to grow, the starfish strips the coral bare until only a white skeleton of dead coral remains.

About thirty years ago, scientists noticed that the population of these starfish was increasing. Large groups of them began feeding on reefs in the Pacific Ocean and on Australia's Great Barrier Reef.

Some scientists believe that human beings may have caused the problem. One of the few animals that eats the crown-of-thorns is the triton, a large marine snail with a beautiful shell. Shell collectors have reduced the number of tritons in the sea, and this may have allowed the crown-of-thorns to increase in number. Other scientists think that population explosions such as this one occur from time to time as part of a natural cycle.

◀ A crown-of-thorns feeds on the polyps of a stony coral. The crown-of-thorns has sixteen arms, each covered with prickly spines.

Each crown-of-thorns can devour about 22 square feet (2 sq m) of coral. In the space of two and a half years, thousands of them destroyed almost all the living coral along a 24-mile (38-km) stretch of reef surrounding the Pacific island of Guam. Areas of Australia's Great Barrier Reef are now in danger.

MAKE A CORAL REEF

Make your own miniature coral reef and watch the fish swim back and forth and then disappear.

You will need:
- three pieces of thin cardboard
- felt-tip pens or paint
- scissors
- glue

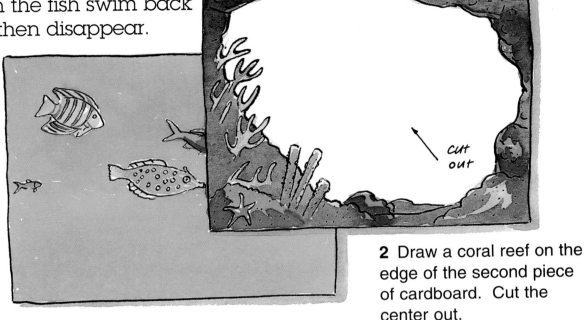

1 Color one piece of cardboard blue for the sea, and draw some fish swimming in the sea.

2 Draw a coral reef on the edge of the second piece of cardboard. Cut the center out.

3 Draw a fish on the third piece of cardboard.

glue

4 Cut out the fish shape and glue it onto a long, narrow strip of cardboard you have colored blue.

5 Place the piece of cardboard with the coral reef on it on top of the blue cardboard. Glue the two pieces of cardboard together, gluing along the top and bottom edges only.

6 Push the long strip of cardboard with the fish between the two larger pieces of cardboard. Pull it back and forth and watch the fish move and then disappear behind the coral.

glue

DANGER FROM PEOPLE

Many of the world's coral reefs are popular tourist attractions. Tourist boats **pollute** the water with gasoline and oil. People who dive down to a reef may damage the coral by stepping on it or scraping it with their diving tanks. Others may break off pieces of coral to take home, although this practice of collecting coral is now illegal in most places.

Overfishing is another problem. If too many fish are taken from one reef or one part of a reef, then the whole balance of life on the reef can change. In some parts of the Caribbean, the algae could not be kept under control because so many algae-eating fish were taken from the sea by fishermen. The algae swamped the coral, and the reef died.

Sewage from towns and cities and poisonous waste materials

▼ Many corals, such as this huge brain coral, have been damaged by tourists.

▲ Tourists buy painted coral gathered from the Great Barrier Reef.

from factories may end up in the water surrounding a coral reef. The dirtier and more polluted the water becomes, the more difficult it is for coral polyps to survive.

Sometimes people clear areas of land near a coastline to make room for crops or houses. The soil washes into the sea, covering the coral with a layer of mud that blocks out the sunlight. The zooxanthellae, which provide the coral polyps with nourishment, die, and so the polyps die. The reef is then deserted by all the other living creatures that depended on it for food and shelter.

DID YOU KNOW?

● Every weekday, about 3,000 people visit the coral reefs in Pennekamp Coral Reef State Park in Florida. On warm summer weekends, that number may rise to 6,000 per day! Between 1984 and 1989, the amount of damage to the coral increased by 300 percent as tourists swarmed to Pennekamp. Some of the reefs may now have to be closed to visitors to allow the coral time to recover.

SCIENCE AT WORK

Marine biologists study the plants and animals living in the sea. They learn many things about human life from these various life forms. Studies of sea urchins, for example, provide information about the way a human baby grows and develops inside his or her mother's womb. Experiments on squids may help us understand how messages are sent from the human brain to different parts of the body.

▲ This platform has been set up as a base for marine biologists studying the reef.

Many sea creatures produce substances that are helpful to human beings.

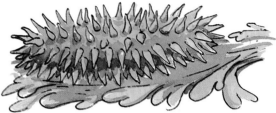

Corals, sponges, sea cucumbers, and seaweed all contain materials that can be used to treat illnesses, including cancer.

Some sponges produce substances that can be used to treat skin infections, food and blood poisoning, and pneumonia.

The poisons produced from certain kinds of shellfish and puffer fish are powerful **anesthetics**, far more powerful than the drugs doctors now give their patients.

Marine biologists believe that many of these materials will eventually be used to make medicines.

▶ Divers mark off an area of reef for close marine study.

SHIPWRECK!

The storm had been raging for three days. At first we were allowed to help the adults on deck, but since the *Seaspray*'s mast had broken yesterday, we had been told to stay in the cabin. My sister Carrie would not stop crying, and,

to tell the truth, I was cold, wet, and miserable enough to want to do the same. But my mother had told me to look after the kids while the adults handled things on deck, so I did as she asked.

Suddenly the cabin door flew open and my mother came in. She banged the door behind her, shutting out the darkness and howling wind, and stood there in

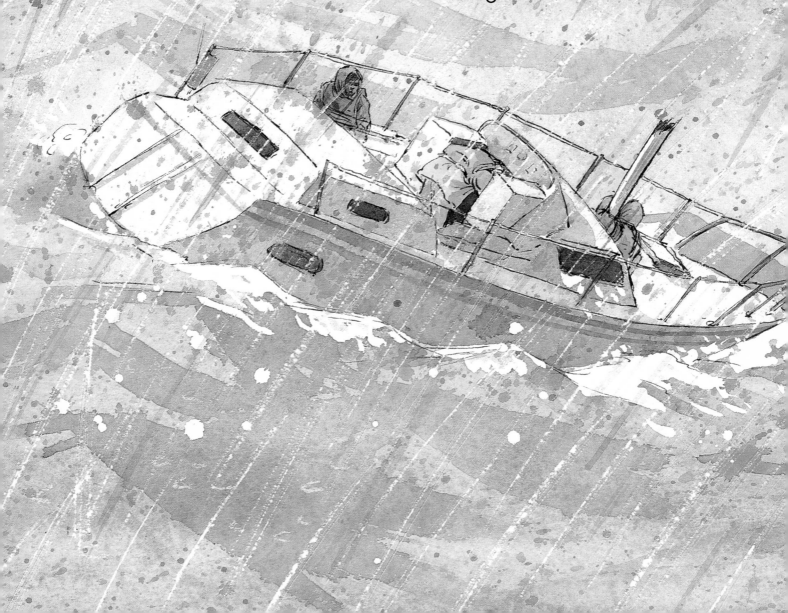

her dripping yellow raincoat.

"Now listen carefully," she began. "Dad thinks we're about to hit a reef, so we'll have to be ready to abandon ship."

She turned to me. "Sue, you're in charge. Gather some food and the first-aid kit. As soon as I call, everyone come up on deck. And hang on to one another!"

My mother turned quickly and opened the door into the howling winds of the storm. Huge drops of rain flew into the room as she left to go back on deck.

I managed to gather some supplies and help Carrie and Luke into their life jackets. Then I heard a booming noise and felt a grinding thud. My mother's shout to us sounded very faint, but I hurried the kids up on deck. The wind and rain whipped around us, but the boat lay still, stuck firmly on the coral.

My father had let the raft down on the sheltered side of the *Seaspray*, and Luke's mother was already in it, ready to help us down. Quickly, we all got in, and Dad pushed off from the yacht and zipped the raft's cover over us.

For a while the raft tossed and turned like a roller coaster. Then, suddenly, the water became still.

"We must have reached the lagoon," said Dad.

He unzipped the cover of the raft, and, in the moonlight, we could see a white beach before us. The wind and rain continued, but the water, sheltered from the ocean current by the reef, was quite calm. My father unclipped the oars, and he and my mother rowed toward the moonlit shore.

The next morning, I awoke to find myself on a magnificent beach. The dazzling white sand was lined with palm trees, and the sun shone on the clear blue waves.

Dad was already up and about.

"Come on!" he called to me. "Let's see what it's like."

We walked inland, where the ground rose steadily into a high hill. From the top of the hill, we could see the whole island, surrounded by the peaceful lagoon and then the ridge of coral. Beyond that lay the Pacific Ocean, tossing up white waves against the coral. I could hardly believe that this now-peaceful expanse of water was the same that had ripped our yacht to pieces only yesterday.

"Wow!" I said. "We're real, live castaways!"

"Not for long, I hope," said Dad. "I managed to send out a distress call before we abandoned ship. But, in the meantime, let's enjoy this adventure."

"Hey, Carrie, Luke," I yelled, as I ran back down to the beach. "Let's go look for buried treasure!"

TRUE OR FALSE?

**Which of the statements below are true and which are false?
If you have read this book carefully, you will know the answers.**

1 There are four basic different types of coral reef.

2 Most fish that live in and around a coral reef have brightly colored bodies.

3 Scientists who study life in the sea are called marine biologists.

4 The polyps that build coral reefs are known as soft corals.

5 Most coral reefs are located in cold ocean waters.

6 A barrier reef is separated from the shore by an area of calm water called a lagoon.

7 Sponges are a common type of underwater plant.

8 The effects of tourism are destroying many of the world's coral reefs.

9 Coral polyps capture food by using the stinging cells on their tentacles.

10 An atoll is a type of fish.

11 The crown-of-thorns is a type of coral polyp that eats starfish.

12 Many of the creatures and plants that live in and around a coral reef depend on each other for food and shelter.

Answers: 1 False; **2** True; **3** True; **4** False; **5** False; **6** True; **7** False; **8** True; **9** True; **10** False; **11** False; **12** True

GLOSSARY

Algae are tiny water plants that provide food for many sea creatures. There are about 25,000 different types of algae.

Anesthetics are drugs used in medicine to prevent a person from feeling pain. Anesthetics work by causing loss of feeling in an area of the body or in the entire body. The effects of an anesthetic usually last for only a short time.

Barrier reef is a type of coral reef separated from a shoreline by an area of calm water called a lagoon.

Cells are sometimes called "units of life." All living things are made up of cells. Some animals and plants have only one cell; others are made up of many cells. In many-celled creatures, each cell has a particular job to do.

Coral atoll is a ring-shaped coral reef surrounding a lagoon. Coral atolls may develop into coral islands as trees and plants begin to grow from seeds carried by the wind, by birds, or on ocean currents.

Crust is the name given to the earth's thin surface layer. It is made up of huge, thick slabs of rock called plates that float on the hot, liquid rock of the mantle below.

Currents are movements of water, each traveling in a particular direction. There are many currents in the world's oceans.

Fringe reef is a type of coral reef that forms a border, or fringe, of coral along a shoreline. A fringe reef is separated from the land by a narrow stretch of water.

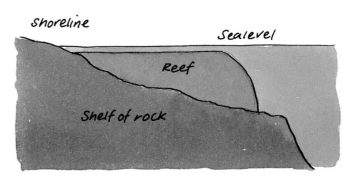

Habitat is the natural home of a plant or animal — the place where something or someone usually lives.

Lagoon is a calm, shallow body of water that is either near or connected to a larger body of water.

Planula is a single, young coral polyp. The plural form of this word is *planulae*.

Pollute means to make something dirty. Earth's water is being polluted by all the human and industrial waste that is dumped into rivers, lakes, and seas.

Sewage is water that contains human waste. Most sewage eventually flows into rivers, lakes, or seas. In many countries, sewage is treated beforehand to remove harmful chemicals and bacteria. But in some countries, sewage is not treated, and so the rivers, lakes, and seas are polluted. This causes harm to the creatures that live there as well as to humans.

Species is the word used to describe a group of animals or plants that share similar characteristics.

Sperm are male sex cells that, when joined with female sex cells, are capable of producing offspring.

Spicules are tiny needles of limestone that strengthen the bodies of soft corals.

Tentacles are the flexible, tubelike parts of a coral polyp's body that surround its mouth and are primarily used to collect food. Other sea creatures, such as sea anemones, also have tentacles.

Volcanic island is an island formed by an underwater volcano. Each time the volcano erupts, it grows in size until its tip lies above sea level. The tip of the volcano is called the volcanic island.

Zooplankton are tiny creatures that float through the water and are eaten by coral polyps.

Zooxanthellae are a type of algae that live inside the bodies of coral polyps and provide them with nourishment. Zooxanthellae use energy from sunlight to make food, and so they must live in clear, shallow water where the sunlight can reach them.

INDEX